Millennials!
Your Secret Weapon to Kick Ass in the Marketplace

Brett Dillon

Copyright © 2018 Brett Dillon. All rights reserved.

No part of this publication may be reproduced, distributed, or transmitted in any form or by any means, including photocopying, recording, or other electronic or mechanical methods, without the prior written permission of the copyright holder, except in the case of brief quotations embodied in reviews and certain other non-commercial uses permitted by US copyright law.

ISBN: 1729737803

ISBN-13: 9781729737804

I dedicate this book to Donovan, Connor, Alastair, Chandler, Ora, Alyssa, and Heather— you taught me how to lead Millennials.

Thanks to my mentors: John Icenogle, Kevin Fitzpatrick, Ralph Wise, Ben Rosson, Bill Scheer, Adrian Street, Mike Barcik, Bob McNutt, Ross Bacon, Charles Ballard, Paul Martinelli, Roddy Galbraith, Mike Braten, Christian Simpson, Mark Cole, and John Maxwell..and my dad, Jimmy Dillon.

I wouldn't be who I am today without my wife, Dina.

Finally—to all the business leaders and the Millennials they lead, I salute you! If you follow my advice, you can create a sustainable competitive advantage in your operating space...and have fun doing it.

Introduction	3
The Generations	7
9 Things We Have in Common	11
12 Ways We Are Different	14
Myths & Misconceptions	18
Myth: Millennials Lack a Work Ethic	20
Misconception: Millennials Are Lazy	24
Decision Point	30
Purpose	35
Purpose	36
How to Live a Meaningless Life	40
How to Discover Purpose	49
How to Live a Life of Purpose	55
Get Good	62
Get Good	63
How to Become Mediocre	67
How to Get Good	70
Workplace Mentor	72
Deliberate Practice	79
Challenging Work	83
Deliberate Performance	86
Get Good Wrap-up	88
Take Responsibility & Give Accountability	89

Take Responsibility & Give Accountability 90

How to Avoid Responsibility & Accountability ... 93

How to Take Responsibility & Give Accountability ... 96

Conclusion ... 100

Suggested Reading ... 103

About the Author ... 108

PART ONE

THE PROBLEM IN THE WORKFORCE

Introduction

Introduction

Do you struggle to lead Millennials? Do you look at your Millennial workforce and wonder how on earth you can win in your marketplace? Do you feel stuck with a generation of workers who just can't seem to get it together?

This insightful and entertaining book will teach you how to win in your marketplace with a secret weapon: your Millennials!

I teach you how to turn your Millennials into a kick ass team through 3 workforce interventions. Along the way, you will learn about work ethics (and how to spot people likely to have a strong one) and how to change a culture of overwork.

If you're like many business leaders and managers, you struggle with how to recruit employees who are engaged with their work, retain talented employees, increase productivity, help your people gain rare and valuable skills, establish a culture of accountability, and most of all— how to turn your Millennial workforce into a winning secret weapon.

Let's face the brutal truth: your people are your only unique, sustainable competitive advantage and differentiator in your operating space—learn how to develop your human capital for maximum effect!

This book will show you how with proven strategies and tactics. I have successfully deployed these interventions in my own life, and in the businesses and volunteer organizations I've led over the years.

I've spent the last decade figuring Millennials out...and gained uncomfortable insights along the way, insights I will share with you.

The first time I hired a Millennial was in 2007. She was a brilliant mechanical engineer— aced the interviews, was a great hire. She had graduated from university and was eager to show what she knew.

The work she did involved a lot of data entry into engineering software and looking for patterns, anomalies, and doing energy load analysis— real nerdy, technology driven stuff.

Her phone was always on her desk and it would buzz about every 7-10 minutes. As soon as it would go off, she would pick it up, read the text, respond to it, and then shift back into work.

She was fast, but when I checked her error rates they were just under the limit.

I had another guy that was on that team. He was a couple of years younger than me, detail oriented, not quite as fast, but he had an extremely low error rate.

Annual review time came around and I talked with her about the challenges we had with her task-shifting and the error rate. She started to tear up and cry— and this is when it hit me that there was a real difference between us— how we viewed ourselves, our relationship with work, and in this case how we receive feedback.

The Millennial generation has entered the workforce and are different from previous generations in their expectations from employers.

In the last 10 years, research indicates this is a worldwide challenge— but also reveals three workplace interventions that are proven to increase employee engagement.

I lead a consulting firm and over half of my employees are Millennials, so I have a vested interest in learning and applying the lessons culled from the evidence produced by the research. The evidence suggests that employee engagement is at an all-time low, with nearly 25% of your employees sabotaging your business—while you pay them to do so!

These three workplace interventions have worked to increase positive employee engagement everywhere they have been deployed.

From large multinational firms to small, family owned businesses, these three interventions improve productivity and effectiveness, increasing the return on your human capital investment.

Because your competitive advantage lies in your people, your human capital, you must deploy these three interventions for your business to thrive in the 21st century.

Join me on this journey of discovery as we reveal the three interventions needed to engage and lead your Millennial workforce.

The Generations

The Generations

As I go through these descriptions, check them against your experience and see if they ring true.

Demographically, Boomers are the generation born between 1946 and 1964 and represent about 44 million people in the workforce. Generation X is the generation born between 1965 and 1979 and represents about 53 million people in the workforce. The Millennials are the generation born between 1980 and 2000 and represent the largest generation in US history. They are rapidly becoming the largest generational demographic in the workforce.

Psychographically, Boomers have a deep reaction to traditions. They tend to be more self-absorbed than the other generations and have a strong drive for personal recognition and fulfillment. They also have a hunger for personal wealth and material gain— a strong consumerism philosophy.

The Boomers gave us desegregation, rock-n-roll, and women in the workforce. As a generational cohort, their attitude is optimistic. They believe in possibilities and are idealistic about how they can make a positive difference in the world. They also tend to be very competitive and look for ways to change the system to get ahead (The Kobayashi Maru incident, for example).

They were influenced by Dr. Martin Luther King, Jr., John F. Kennedy, Gloria Steinem, and The Beatles. Places such as Kent

State and the Hanoi Hilton resonate with this group. Television had a profound impact on their world. They were raised to believe they could change the world, and that anything was possible.

They get a tremendous amount of personal gratification from their work and believe in self-improvement and personal growth.

Generation X is the most misunderstood, most ignored generation. They are the first generation that didn't do better than the previous one, and the first one raised with both parents working. They have rising divorce rates.

They have a strong entrepreneurial drive, perhaps related to the changes in corporate attitudes to the workforce. They seek truth to counter the hype we are constantly exposed to and try to achieve work-life balance. They are independent, resourceful, and tend to be reluctant to have anyone help them out.

The smallest generational cohort, they saw the likes of Bill Clinton, Al Bundy, Madonna, Beavis & Butthead, and Dennis Rodman make headlines during their formative years. Their world changed shape with the fall of the Soviet Union, the rise of global terrorism, and the flooding of the world with data available on the Internet. This is the generation that is defined by media and technology.

Their codeword is skepticism and they tend to put more faith in the individual than in any institution, whether marriage or their employer. They are aware of diversity and tend to think globally. They try to balance work with the rest of their life, often to no avail.

They tend to be informal and practical in their approach to work.

The Millennials are the most diverse, most educated, most marketed to, most cared for, most medicated, and most maligned generation. Nearly half have been raised by divorced parents and a third lived with a single parent. Three-fourths of this generation had a working mother.

They are the digital natives, growing up in times of rapid technology shifts and social change. They face insecurity combined with affluence. More than 95% of this generation are on social media, perhaps as a way to get a stronger sense of community through digital instead of human interactions.

They are a very impatient generation, often demanding immediate responses. They appreciate diversity, prefer collaboration to being ordered, and are pragmatic when solving problems. They view themselves as being realistic and have a strong sense of confidence in their skills, a confidence that may not be based competence.

They grew up with Prince William, Winky Tinky, Venus and Serena Williams, and Britney Spears. They witnessed the Columbia disaster, the destruction of the Twin Towers on September 11, and the murders at Columbine.

Raised by optimistic Boomers, Millennials feel empowered to take positive action when things go wrong, even if their action is only symbolic. They have a heightened sense of moral outrage at perceived injustices, and believe in service to the community.

When I gave that annual review to the first Millennial I hired, you can probably see why she had such an emotional reaction—and why I was confused by it. She had wrapped her worth in her perception of what others think, common for those with high social media usage, and was affected by corrective feedback—combined with the delay in giving her feedback caused her to wonder why I didn't talk to her earlier. Her work was within the limits, so I didn't see a need for an intervention—but from her perspective, I had failed her.

9 Things We Have in Common

9 Things We Have in Common

According to the IBM Institute for Business Value, here are the ways these generations are alike, within 5 percentage points. Of course, the answers you get from research surveys are dependent on the questions asked.

1. Make a positive impact on my organization. Millennials (25%), Generation X (21%), and Boomers (23%) have the long-term goal of positively impacting their organization. They all want to create a legacy.
2. Help solve social and environmental challenges. Millennials (22%), Generation X (20%), and Boomers (24%) want to work on big problems that impact their communities and society at large.
3. Work with a diverse group of people. Millennials (22%), Generation X (22%), and Boomers (21%) want to work with people who are different from themselves, who have different lifestyles and perspectives.
4. Work for an organization considered among the best in the industry. Millennials (21%), Generation X (25%), and Boomers (23%) want to work for an organization with a great reputation in their industry.
5. Do work they are passionate about. Millennials (20%), Generation X (21%), and Boomers (23%) have all fallen prey to the Passion Trap and want to do work they love.
6. Become an expert in their field. Millennials (20%),

Generation X (20%), and Boomers (15%) want to become recognized as experts in their field of interest.
7. Manage work-life balance. Millennials (18%), Generation X (22%), and Boomers (21%) have a career goal of balance between business and life.
8. Become a senior leader. Millennials (18%), Generation X (18%), and Boomers (18%) desire positions of senior leadership in their organizations.
9. Achieve financial security. Millennials (17%), Generation X (16%), and Boomers (18%) want to achieve financial security as a long-term career goal.

We are alike in many of the drivers of personal achievement, perhaps more alike than we'd care to admit sometimes.

But because we are humans, we like to figure out how we are different from others. We use these differences to exclude others from our tribe and weight those differences based on our needs. Are those differences enough to warrant exclusion, or do we need some resources from them that justifies inclusion in our tribe?

12 Ways We Are Different

12 Ways We Are Different

Here are 12 criteria that have generational differences. As I go through them, check my descriptions against your own experience and see if they ring true for you.
1. Level of trust. Millennials have high levels of trust toward authority—but they determine who the authority is. Generation X tends to have low levels of trust toward authority, having witnessed political and religious scandals on a regular basis. Boomers are confident in themselves, but tend to have less confidence in authority figures.
2. Loyalty to institutions. Millennials are committed to the institutions that have been part of their lives, while Generation X is considered naive when dealing with institutions. Boomers, on the other hand, tend to be cynical about institutions.
3. Who they admire. Millennials want to follow a hero of integrity (their definition of integrity may differ than the other generations, as might their definition of hero). Generation X admires those who create enterprises, and Boomers admire those who take charge.
4. Careers. Millennials want to build parallel careers, working in the gig economy as freelancers or moonlighting. Generation X wants to build portable careers, having seen the loss of corporate loyalty to the workforce. Boomers want to build a stellar career.

5. Rewards. Millennials feel rewarded by doing meaningful work, while Generation X gets the sense of reward from the freedom to not do things. Boomers tend to feel rewarded by titles and prime office space, signaling everyone in the organization their status.
6. Parent-Child Involvement. Millennials' parents tend to be intruders, the classic helicopter parent, always hovering nearby. Generation X parents tended to be distant, and Boomers parents tended to recede into the background.
7. Children. Millennials are definite about children, and have decided whether they will or will not have any and how many they will have (if they have decided to have any). Generation X tended to be doubtful about children, while Boomers tended to be controlled.
8. Family life. Millennials were protected as children. Generation X tended to be alienated as children, and Boomers were indulged as children—perhaps as a way to compensate for the receding parenting they received.
9. Education. Millennials demand a structure of accountability from educational systems. Generation X tends to be pragmatic about education, seeking it only if it proves useful. For Boomers, education is the path to freedom of expression.
10. Evaluation. Millennials want feedback whenever they want it, a nearly constant stream of letting them know how they are doing in some cases. Generation X tends to feel apologetic when they ask for feedback and Boomers want feedback once a year with documentation.
11. Political orientation. Millennials crave community and follow political ideals and politicians who promise connections that support community creation and maintenance. Generation X tends to be apathetic politically, focusing on individual rights and voting outside party lines for individuals. Boomers tend to be opposed to oppression, whether from our government or others.

12. The big question. For Millennials, the big question of their life is "How do we build it?" Generation X, ever the pragmatic generation, asks "Does it work?" Boomers ask "What does it mean?"

Myths & Misconceptions

Myths & Misconceptions

Since my first meaningful encounter with a Millennial in the workforce in 2007, I have seen other differences, differences that have a profound impact on workforce relations and generational perceptions.

The first time I noticed this other set of differences that appear to be generational (but aren't) happened when we had a lot of work come in— we would need to get a lot done in a compressed time frame. Imagine my surprise when our Millennial employee, who was salaried, left the office at 5 pm while I kept working. I noticed this happened a lot—I would be working nights and weekends to get the work done, but the Millennials would pack up and leave at the end of their shift. I associated their behavior with their generation, but it turns out… I was wrong.

There were two things at play here, one a myth and the other a misconception.

Myth: Millennials Lack a Work Ethic

Before we get into work ethic differences, let me describe what the elements of a work ethic are.

Good work ethics include interpersonal skills, initiative, and dependability. The key interpersonal skills necessary for a good work ethic are empathy, courteousness, friendliness, cheerfulness, considerate, pleasant, cooperative, helpful, likable, devoted, loyal, well-groomed, patient, appreciative, hard-working, modest, emotionally stable, and stubbornness.

Initiative requires the person to be perceptive, productive, resourceful, proactive, ambitious, efficient, effective, enthusiastic, dedicated, persistent, accurate, conscientious, independent, adaptable, persevering, and orderly.

Dependability describes a person who follows directions and regulations, is dependable, reliable, careful, honest, and punctual.

Bad work ethics are held by people who are hostile, rude, selfish, devious, irresponsible, careless, negligent, depressed, tardy, and apathetic.

This is the tale of two work ethics and a collision of cultures that will have a profound impact on education and business.

The classical work ethic was developed several hundred years ago during a period of almost universal scarcity and deprivation. The choices were to work hard or starve—so those who didn't work hard were removed from the gene pool.

This work ethic, also known as the Protestant Work Ethic, was cemented into the European middle class about 200 years ago.

This work ethic explains poverty as the logical consequence of idleness and poor money management. Wealth is explained by hard work, honest work, and saving money. Unemployment is caused by laziness and lack of effort and ambition.

This yields these perspectives on work: Work is a fact of life, life is hard, so you have a duty to work hard. If you maintain a rational attitude toward life, use good time management skills, your effortful diligence will lead to success. And success is important—so consumption and leisure should be treated with some suspicion. However, caring for others and good citizenship are civic duties.

With the rise of the Millennial generation, a new work ethic has shown up: the contemporary work ethic. But this work ethic wasn't created or caused by the Millennials— and the Millennials are often blamed for something they aren't guilty of.

The contemporary work ethic has three causes. The differences between these work ethics may be causing cultural clashes sparked by incompatible perspectives on work and life—perceived incompatible by groups on both sides. But the causes of the contemporary work ethic are born from the classical work ethic—in fact, these three causes would likely not exist if it weren't for the classical work ethic.

The first cause of the contemporary work ethic is affluence. The rapid shift to technology has created wealth to the point that children have the latest smart phones and tablets. This technology driven affluence is creating inequalities that are destroying the middle class.

The second cause is an emphasis on personal growth and fulfillment beyond economic needs. This has shifted the emphasis from work-to-survive to work-to-have-a-life.

The third cause is the attitudes of parents. It turns out that parents pass their attitudes toward class and education to their children.

These yield this perspective on work: your work and regular job should represent your core life motives, causing the people with the contemporary work ethic to fall prey to the Passion Trap.

A steady job is more significant than leisure time, but this leads to the ethos that one should work, not one must work. Full-time work is one option among many: full-time work or be a professional student, full-time work or do temporary work, full-time work or do part-time work, full-time work or be a freelancer, full-time work or do flexible work, full-time work or do constructive leisure.

These work ethic differences create a cultural clash. We're always looking for differences to exclude others from our tribe, weighting those differences according to whether we need their resources or not. The differences in attitudes toward work seem to be significant.

There are statistically significant and substantially positive correlations between classical work ethics and cultural conservatism. This has an interesting effect when cultural conservatism fades from those with a classical work ethic. The work ethic stays strong, but the focus is on consumerism: one has a duty to work to achieve consumer goals. This twist on the classical work ethic has all the Protestant Work Ethic perspectives except the depreciative attitude toward leisure time.

Education also has an impact on work ethic. There is a linear decrease in work ethics as education increases. The working class, less privileged, and poor youth do not view education as a lever to promote them through a career. In fact, the very notion of a career reflects to them a middle class bias of how to proceed through working life. They believe they are probably destined to the lower levels of the occupational system. They know it takes effort to find and keep a job.

Because of these beliefs, they armor themselves with a strong work ethic. They feel they need to work at all costs, they need to work just to get by, and leisure activities are fine as long as your occupational status is safe.

Middle and upper class youth view higher education as an obvious requirement to make it into the higher levels of the occupational system. They tend to be more casual about the importance and worth of work.

As we see the explosion of urban growth, we also see a decline in cultural conservatism and an increase in education and affluence concentrated in urban areas. The 2016 US Presidential election illustrates this.

The contemporary work ethic is not a generational thing—it is conflated with Millennials, but created by affluence, a focus on personal growth, and parental attitudes toward social class.

Lack of work ethics, whether classical or contemporary, has an established inverse relationship with the level of education. As formal education levels go up, work ethics go down. Lack of work ethics are also related to higher population densities and culturally liberal parental views.

Misconception: Millennials Are Lazy

I would get frustrated when these talented employees would leave at 5 pm while we had so much work to get done. I had a problem. I was advised to write them up, give them poor performance reviews, to force them to work my way—or fire them and hire someone who would do what is required to get the job done.

I struggled with this advice because they were soooo talented! How could I write them up when they were working the hours we had agreed to? How could I give a poor performance review when their work was good? And I couldn't find anywhere in their job description where I called out drive and ambition as requirements for the job. I had a problem.

My problem was my unhealthy relationship with work. I compared my addiction to work to their perspective on work, and benchmarked them against the culture of overwork I created.

Here's how to create a culture of overwork.

First, don't let employees take scheduled breaks beyond what labor laws require.

Second, insist they see their work get finished. Use the excuses that they will experience the joy of completing a task, or that their self-esteem will improve when they accomplish a goal, or the enforcement side of the coin: they have to pay their dues like we did back in our day.

Third, employ the flip side of the Passion Trap: Love What You Do. A lot of people got Steve Jobs' commencement speech at Stanford University wrong: they think he supported the Passion Trap (Do What You Love), when in fact he espoused the opposite: Love What You Do. In his speech at the 2005 commencement, he stated: "Your work is going to fill a large part of your life and the only way to be truly satisfied is to do what you believe is great work, and the only way to do great work is to love what you do."

The key to love what you do is to do something for a long time and become good at it. Behaviors will always precede emotions. Taken to extremes, this attitude can lead to the Hero Complex which can have the Hero getting in over their head and doing work they are incompetent at (leading to expensive re-work) and a failure to delegate which leads to bottlenecks because the rest of the team doesn't develop the expertise needed to relieve the Hero chokepoint.

Fourth, insist that everyone is always busy. This will lead to a failure to prioritize work so nothing ever gets done, but everyone is tired at the end of the day because they have been busy...ineffective, but efficiently doing lots of things that aren't important.

Fifth, use labor-productivity costs as a key performance indicator so you can drive the wrong behaviors (see the fourth point). It is important to ensure the employees are utilized to their full capacity, even if what they produce isn't needed or wanted by customers.

I had a problem with all the Millennials leaving at 5 pm while I was working nights and weekends. But that was a problem with me. I chose to stay late and work on weekends. That was my choice, not theirs. I had to look at myself—how could I hold them responsible for my choices?

I had to look at the evidence-based research I've accumulated over the past 10 years, and when I did—I discovered it was irrational for me to expect anything else. I had unrealistic expectations and had fallen prey to confirmation bias: their different choices were due to laziness, not because I had an unhealthy relationship with work.

To overcome my problem, I had to shift the culture at work—and that started with shifting my relationship with work.

The first issue I had to deal with was breaks. I started to have conversations with my staff about common interests outside of work…what a concept! I encouraged discussions about what we did over the weekend, where we went out to eat, what films or television shows we watched. I paid for gym memberships for the staff and encouraged them to go whenever they felt they needed to—even if that was during the day.

I modeled taking naps in the afternoon, made a point of telling everyone I was taking a nap (I still do). I encouraged them to take naps. I made a rule that we could only work for 50 minutes, then we had to take a 10 minute break during which we could listen to music, surf the web, goof off on social media, or walk around outside. I insisted we wouldn't work through lunch—and often, I would take them out to lunch to prevent them from doing so. We agreed we wouldn't eat where we worked (although I still have a hard time enforcing that one—some of my staff are obstinate).

I made meditation resources available to everyone, practiced mindfulness meditation throughout the day, and encouraged everyone else to do so as well, particularly when things got rocky. We instituted a morning ritual of learning something new, and learning it together—before we tackled the work that needed to be done. I encouraged the expression of gratitude to our colleagues, the behavior of doing something to make someone else happy.

The second issue I tackled was the need to see work finished. We stocked the break room with healthy snacks, such as almonds, apples, oatmeal, and avocados to help get our bodies and minds in a healthy state. Following Bob Sutton's advice in his book The No Asshole Rule, we instituted a "No-Asshole

Rule" to develop a civilized workplace. It's OK to occasionally be an asshole; after all, we are only human. But it is NOT acceptable to engage in a pattern of behavior that indicates one is a certified recidivist asshole. I encourage everyone to read and apply the lessons from his book.

We focused on collaboration instead of competition, cross-functional teams instead of silos, and teamwork, teamwork, teamwork. Mindfulness meditation became a very useful tool to deal with our beliefs that control our behaviors that control our feelings. Self-compassion became the rule rather than the exception.

I had to have repeated conversations with one employee who seemed hell bent on sabotaging herself. She would, on a nearly daily basis, get out of her swim lane and do work she was terrible at, work she was not asked to do—work that would lead to poor performance and a resultant counseling session. I had to remind her to play to her strengths, stay in her lane, trust her colleagues to do the work she saw needed to be done.

I encouraged her to build on her strengths and expand them instead of trying to develop her weaknesses into strengths. We would let her know that self-forgiveness is a real thing—it's OK to make mistakes because that's how we learn, and making mistakes doesn't mean one is stupid. Mistakes are indications we've found out something useful; we learned that we didn't know something as well as we thought we did, found a hole in our knowledge, and now we can go figure out how to fill the knowledge gap.

I provided everyone copies of <u>Daring Greatly</u> by Brene Brown, <u>Mindset</u> by Carol Dweck, <u>Mindfulness</u> by Ellen Langer. We went through each of these books as a team, culling lessons learned and discussing how we would apply the principles to our lives. All of these elements help us understand we are not our work, encourages us to focus on quality instead of quantity, and to live our values.

The third issue I tackled was loving what we do a little bit too much. I had to start with myself: I would pull the classic "It's just easier (or faster or cheaper or whatever excuse you want to use) for me to do it myself!". I had to break my poor work habits which were based on wrapping my identity around my work.

It's a constant area of focus for me now, and a new experience for me to delegate work to my staff. It occurred to me that I hired them for a reason and I should use their knowledge, skills, and abilities—and where they were lacked, I needed to train them. I started by setting clear expectations for the task I needed done, including any weird things I insist on like following a designed process, documentation of work, and my expectations of quality. I started by delegating small chores and tasks and learned to develop staff to delegate tasks as well.

I tend to hire T-shaped people: broad range and depth of expertise and knowledge, with deep expertise in one area we work in. If the work isn't in our lane of expertise, delegate it to someone who is an expert at it. I found that I was the only person required to be a generalist; everyone else needed to be a specialist cross-trained in at least one other area.

This meant I had to let go of having everything done the way I would do it, and focus instead on crafting the mission and my desired outcome for my staff and hold them accountable and responsible to achieve the bigger picture. As long as they operated within our values and principles, we were good to go.

So I had to teach them our values and principles first— we spent a lot of time in discovery to distill what is most important. I delegated recurring tasks, with an eye toward automating the ones we can (once I get over my dislike for technology). I had to learn how to lead by asking great questions more than giving mediocre answers.

One of my favorite leadership questions I learned from one of my mentors, Ross Bacon, was "If you were me, what would you do?". After they responded, I'd tell them they should do that. Their answers were usually way better than any I had rolling around in my head anyway.

I also had to teach them the principles of collaboration and teamwork. I would have them work as a team on lots of different types of projects, from self-discovery to video production.

The fourth issue I tackled was our productivity and the cost of labor. It didn't make sense to have people work on projects that weren't valuable for them to do—I needed to leverage their expertise, but I also needed to balance that with staff development; others needed to gain expertise in that area as well. I had to look at what was valuable and define it as something beyond monetary value.

Our leverage wasn't structured around position, but around expertise: if someone else was the expert on a project, I reported to them (even though I sign their paychecks). It may seem unconventional, but it works…if I don't have a huge ego and insist on being the boss.

It turned out, I learned a lot from the front-line and it helped me become a better leader.

Decision Point

Decision Point

Now that I realized that Millennials didn't lack a work ethic and weren't lazy, I had to make a choice. I saw I had three options.

I could force them to adapt to my structures, systems and perspectives. In the US alone, we've spent billions of dollars to get our workforces engaged—and we've wasted billions of dollars trying to get our workforces engaged. Only about 1/3 of our employees are engaged in their work with about 2/3 disengaged...and a large chunk of them are actively disengaged! That means we are paying someone to sabotage our businesses.

So the option of forcing them to adapt to our structures, systems, and perspectives has lots of evidence that indicates it doesn't work.

I could fire the Millennials for being different and never hire another Millennial again. Given the demographics of the workforce, my final employee would lock the company's doors permanently in 2037. So beyond the legal issues, my organization wouldn't survive to the next generation.

And who would we sell our services to? The Millennials are the largest generation our nation has ever seen.

That left me with this: we should adapt our structures, systems and perspectives to fit their needs. And they need to learn some important skills that have not been taught to them.

We also discovered three workplace interventions that are crucial to leading Millennials, with the added benefit that these interventions are beneficial for all generations in the workforce, and the skills they need to learn will help the Millennials live richer, more fulfilling lives. This is a classic Win-Win.

The three workplace interventions are alignment of personal and corporate purposes, becoming good at what we do, and taking responsibility for our actions.

Part Two

The Solutions

Purpose

Purpose

For many years, I struggled with discovering my purpose. I fell into the Passion Trap and pursued careers doing things I loved to do: I worked at a small town police department, as a security officer for an exclusive community, a surveillance operative, a bodyguard, a youth pastor, a professional catch wrestler, a pro wrestler— and I filled in the gaps with doing things I was good at, but not passionate about: carpentry, renovations, and homebuilding.

I was raised on two basic principles when it came to work: first, do everything as if unto the Lord (my mom) and second, make my mom proud (my dad). It didn't have to be perfect, just good enough for God. So whatever I did, I got good at it— whether as passion or a vocation. What I learned was how to quickly and deeply learn a skill and my motivation didn't matter: my work quality did.

It was when I built houses as the Construction Director for the Chattanooga Habitat for Humanity affiliate that I first got a fleeting glimpse of my purpose. As I broke down the construction process to find ways to become more efficient with our resources and more effective at accomplishing our mission, I discovered an unexpected result: lives were being transformed.

I set out to build better houses and ended up helping people become better.

On a Sunday evening in December 2002, one of our

homebuyers tracked me down to my home. In our living room, she showed my wife and I her utility bill for November—her highest one so far. It was $39. Not bad for an all-electric home with a single mom and three kids.

Then she told me what she was doing with this extra cash she now had. She had enrolled in classes at the local college and was studying to become a nurse! For the first time in generations, a cycle of poverty was being broken, children were seeing their mother as a positive role model, and a family was getting their shot at the American Dream.

This is when I realized it wasn't about the bricks and sticks—it was about the families who dwell in the homes. My actions had an impact that went far beyond the limits of my vision of building a better home.

The last time I checked, she was working as a nurse at a teaching hospital.

I went on to work at Southface Energy Institute as the evangelist for their green building program, expanding its sphere of influence throughout the Southeast. Then I went to work for Chattanooga Neighborhood Enterprise in their development department. At each place, I became good at what I did—and expanded into a deeper realization of my purpose.

At the age of 37, I had finally discovered why I was here: to help everyone I meet become better for having met me. It had expanded beyond transforming how my organization built homes, beyond transforming regional homebuilding practices, beyond transforming neighborhoods—it was about the transformation of people.

I have since refined my purpose—as I have learned a few lessons along the way. By the way, I will always learn new things. The more I learn, the more I realize how little I know. My refined purpose is to help those who hunger for their destiny to become the best versions of themselves.

This personal purpose drives our business purpose to help clients become the best versions of themselves in the marketplace through education, media production, quality management, competitive insights, and leadership development.

Purpose must never be confused for passion—nor passion for purpose. Lots of people are passionate about things they are ill-designed for, and so set off to pursue what they love and achieve mediocre results. Purpose is not the same thing as passion, and purpose trumps passion—particularly in the beginning.

Too many people think the stuff in their life they are passionate about indicates their purpose—sometimes it does, more often it does not.

Purpose is important because it provides focus. It is the lens of our life that frames what is important and what isn't. Our purpose frames why we exist, where we fit in our world, and why we matter.

Carl Jung said, "Man cannot stand a meaningless life."

For businesses, our corporate purpose drives our talent recruitment, the discretionary effort of our employees, and employee retention. Show me an organization with high employee turnover and I'll show you how they failed to connect corporate and individual purposes.

Organizations are groups of people who have agreed to work together for a common purpose. That purpose must be made known and relevant to every single member of the organization for it to become effective in fulfilling that purpose.

Too often companies declare their purpose as some sort of inspirational slogan. This is stupid and insulting. When I drink bottled water, I'm doing it because it is conveniently packaged hydration, not because I want to have an inspired moment of optimism and happiness! I'm thirsty and it's handy.

How does an inspiring moment of optimism and happiness connect with the operator on the bottling line? Do they get up every morning inspired to work at the plant because they are going to help some unknown person on the planet have an inspired moment of optimism and happiness? Does that drive any discretionary effort above and beyond their wage agreement?

Or would it be better to declare their purpose is to provide clean, safe drinking water in convenient packaging so people around the world can have access to an essential requirement for health? Which is more likely to stimulate the best performance of the bottling line operator, the forklift driver, the bottle maker, the sales reps, and the plant supervisors and managers?

The purposes of the organization and individual must be authentic and clear.

Rather than first tell you how to do this—I will describe how not to do it. I know, because I have made most of these mistakes myself. The ones I haven't made, I've observed up close and learned the lesson (I hope).

How to Live a Meaningless Life

The first step to live a meaningless life is to live the life of a conformist. Never have your own opinion, shaped after a personal exploration of deep, insightful thoughts about the issues. Instead, you should agree with your peers and parrot what you've read or seen or heard from social media, the news media, and your friends and family.

Conform to their expectations and for heaven's sake, don't say or do or believe anything different from the herd.

The second step to live a meaningless life is to stop learning as soon as you can. It's important, if one is going to live a meaningless life, that you stop growing what you know as soon as possible. It's preferable that you stop learning as soon as the government will let you, but if you can't stop there, stop as soon as you've learned enough to earn enough—master the basics, but learn nothing beyond that.

One trick to learn as little as possible is to have the answers memorized. What answers? The answers to the questions others ask you, of course! While the trick is to have the answers memorized, the key to not learning is to never ask your own questions.

You must rely on the questions of others—the questions in the book, the questions on the test, the questions from the teacher. And if the teacher does their job to help you live a meaningless life, they will only ask you questions that align with the test, which of course are taken word for word from the book or their boring content.

The third step to live a meaningless life is to make sure you set limits on what you are capable of. If you've followed Steps One and Two, this is easy and if you haven't followed those steps—well, you better go back and conform to the herd and stop learning. You are already in danger of living a life of purpose so you better back off and dial down your ambition.

OK, I'm assuming that you followed instructions now and are ready to set limits on what you can do, what your potential is. To set these limits, you must first believe that you are not in control of your life.

If you are a conformist, this part is easy. You've already given control of your life over to the influence of your peers on social media, allowed the news media to tell you what to think, and how you are—the condition you are in—is someone else's fault. You should first blame your parents, then your teachers. If that doesn't work, blame the government, coworkers, your neighbors, your friends, family—especially your spouse or children.

Children are a good source to blame—after all, think of all the fun you would have had if you hadn't had kids! Think of the money that you would have spent on yourself, making yourself happy, if the rug rats weren't always costing you money. And when you blame someone else for your circumstances, be sure to let them know they are the ones responsible for what has happened to you—but don't tell them. For some reason, they tend to get upset—so drop broad hints that everything is their fault.

After you've accepted you are not in control of your life, you need to reinforce that you aren't worth much to anyone.

The best way to do this is to tell yourself, out loud as often as you can, how much you screw everything up—and by you, of course I mean how everyone around you makes you screw everything up.

The second way to limit your worth is to do things you aren't very good at. This way, other people will tell you how you screw things up which serves two functions: one, you get the reinforcement that you aren't worth much and two, you get to blame them for ruining your self-esteem which reinforces your victimhood.

The third way you can limit your potential is to make sure you stay away from people who don't judge you, the kind of people who might see value in you and what you bring to the table. In fact, I would avoid those people like a syphilitic whore.

The fourth step to living a meaningless life is to make sure you never, ever, under any circumstances, consider what you value. The character traits you need are at the extremes of virtues—this ensures you can fall prey to whatever is popular. Having values that shift with the changing of what is popular is critical to a meaningless life.

But even more important, don't know what you believe to begin with and never question why you believe anything. "Just because..." is the answer that works best if you are ever questioned about these things. Accept whatever your friends say they believe and never think about these things again.

Character traits, values, ethics—don't waste any time or energy thinking about yours. Now of course, you must consider everyone else's, especially if they are different from what your friends think—because different is the same as wrong. And wrong deserves ridicule, especially when you can do it through technology at a safe distance.

Never ridicule someone in person, to their face—they might point out a flaw in your argument or worse. They might turn the tables on you! So don't do it...but if you do, make sure it is a coordinated attack of ridicule through a group of your friends.

It is important to drown out anyone who disagrees with you, so lots of loud people who agree with you is helpful. Don't engage in debate—shout slogans you've heard from others, that may or may not be appropriate. In fact, if the slogans you shout are not relevant, that's even better because the person who is wrong will get confused.

So don't know what you believe and why and drown out everyone who disagrees with what your herd believes.

The fifth step to live a meaningless life is to make sure you only watch, read, and listen to things that entertain you without causing you to think. This is important because your eyes and ears are the portals to your mind and are the chief way to program your thinking—and the more trivial your thinking, the easier it is to live a meaningless life.

I advise you to avoid books unless they are romance novels (women) or adventure novels (men). Magazines that focus on famous people are OK, but stay away from magazines that focus on any important issues.

You should only watch reality TV shows, because everyone knows those shows depict how the world works. And never listen to anything that makes you think—podcasts can be dangerous to living a meaningless life, as can any educational programs such as those found on PBS.

Popular music is a safe choice, and works well to help you prove to your peers how conforming you are. After all, your aim is to be average, so you should only listen to what everyone in your little world listens to. Make sure you only focus on the trivial, entertaining things to watch, read, and listen to so you never risk the programming in your mind getting an unexpected update that might make you think clear and deep.

The sixth step to live a meaningless life is to make it all about you. After all, this is your life so it should be all about you, shouldn't it? Your life should be focused on you—especially on how you feel, how others make you feel, what you want to feel, how you want others to make you feel. After all, if you want to reinforce the systems to provide a meaningless life, it should be based on your feelings and how outside forces in your life make you feel.

This will give you the "right" to be offended by whatever

makes you experience negative emotions, and the more offended you are by what others do and say, the more you are living an emotion-driven meaningless life. Your level of outrage and offense taken is a good marker of how well you are succeeding at living a life without purpose. The real key to this step is to make sure that everything you experience revolves around you and your feelings—and to let everyone within earshot know.

Stay on the emotional roller coaster in your carnival of life—and make sure you sit in the first carriage.

The seventh step to live a meaningless life is to never set goals. When you fail to reach your goals, you will feel terrible about yourself and that will damage your self-esteem. Goals are for people with drive and ambition—two things that will take you out of your meaningless existence.

The first problem with goals is you feel terrible when you don't reach them. You've failed—and everyone knows failure hurts. The second problem with goals: in spite of all your lack of effort to reach them, you might still get there. How? You will find that, on this planet, some people are driven by this insane urge to help other people.

These interfering busybodies will do things that help you achieve your goal—especially when they know you have a goal and see you "struggle" not to reach it. To prevent these so-called do-gooders and helpful people from helping you, don't tell anyone (and I mean anyone) what your goal is. If they don't know, they can't help.

You never know where you will run into these cats, so it is best to keep any concepts of a goal to yourself. Or better yet, never even get a concept of a goal—after all, you can't tell someone something you don't know.

The eighth step to live a meaningless life is to focus on outcomes or results instead of behaviors or actions. A focus on results allows you to conduct yourself however you like as long as "the work gets done". And since most of the outcomes or results in any life depends on the actions of others, a focus on results minimizes your portion of responsibility.

You can blame Joan in accounting for not getting you a specific report on time, or Bob for not closing the three deals needed to make your deal work—with so many cooks in the kitchen, it's easy for meals to get derailed. So focus on results because you get to do whatever you want as long as "it" gets done and when "it" doesn't get done, there is diffused responsibility so it isn't your fault.

The ninth step to live a meaningless life is to contribute as little as possible. When you contribute, you give, not take, and if you give you are actually losing. Contribution to society through volunteering, contribution to your company through your discretionary effort, contribution to your community by paying taxes and voting, all these take time, energy, and money away from the most important thing—you.

Don't share any resources you have, especially if you have more than you need…now. There may be a time in the future when you won't have these things and will need them. Be selfish and hoard all you can of your physical resources and never share your talents or time with anyone.

Giving of yourself will only help them get better, not you—so stay away from situations that expose you to such losses. Contribute as little as possible so you can maximize your accumulation of things—especially things that make you feel good about yourself. There is only one reason to contribute: so you can get recognized for it.

Don't give—but if you do, make sure everyone knows how much you gave so they will give you recognition—which will boost your self-esteem and might lower your taxes.

The tenth step to live a meaningless life is to make sure you aren't fit for much. I've found it is easiest to start with not being physically fit. The important part of not being physically fit is to move as little as possible. You can do this under the guise of being efficient—think of all the time saved by not moving! It's also easier to not move if you stay inside, staring at an electronic screen of some kind—which helps reduce both physical and mental fitness.

The more you use the electronic devices, the less fit your eyes become due to a reduction in your blink rate. It's also helpful to binge watch trivial shows (anything which doesn't make you think deep and clear) on some sort of streaming service—they make it so easy to "stay engaged" with content wherever you are, which encourages you to be sedentary wherever you might be.

The next best trick to staying unfit physically is to understand that if you have to move, do it inside while engaged with machines of some sort. You can even find machines for indoor movement, machines that replicate (sort of) bicycles, walking, and climbing stairs.

Another way to ensure you stay physically unfit is to eat food that is designed to taste great but has low nutritive value. You can do this by eating the inexpensive food available at restaurants designed to deliver the food fast—you can even order, receive, and consume the food without ever leaving the comfort of the vehicle you drove to get to the fast "food" joint.

In addition to being physically unfit, you can become mentally unfit. If you've already followed the advice so far, you are well on your way to becoming mentally unfit. Stop learning as early as possible, never think about what you believe and why, stay attuned to the trivial and entertaining (especially social media), these are all excellent ways to stay mentally unfit.

I've touched on this next tip earlier—but it is so important it deserves more expansive treatment: avoid curiosity. Never ask questions (and if you have to, make sure they are shallow and trivial questions to keep yourself and others from thinking deep and clear) and squash curiosity by accepting whatever the "experts" tell you—and experts can be anyone who has an opinion your peers agree with, regardless of their level of actual expertise in a subject.

An easy way to stop curiosity in its tracks is to remove the word "Why" from your vocabulary. Most people find the use of that word annoying anyway, especially when directed at them, so removal of "Why" serves two purposes: you reduce your curiosity, and improve your popularity. Remember, popularity is more important than rightness, clarity, or authenticity.

To stay spiritually unfit, never consider your place in the multiverse—be confident in not knowing who and what you are, with zero desire to think about these things.

These are the 10 steps to live a meaningless life—but here is one more secret: they work for individuals AND organizations!

1. Conform: for individuals, strive for average; for organizations, rush to sameness with your competitors
2. Stop Learning: for individuals, learn as little as possible; for organizations, don't invest in your people and refuse to capture and share lessons learned by the non-conformists
3. Limit Your Potential: for individuals, set up belief systems that keep you in line with the expectations of average; for organizations, ensure a top-down definition of who you are and what you do based on your current capabilities
4. Don't Know What You Believe and Why: for individuals and organizations, never ask why you exist
5. Focus on the Trivial: for individuals, focus on what others think as expressed through social or news media; for organizations, focus on numbers and metrics that are not aligned with any strategic objective
6. Be Self-Centered: for individuals, make everything about you and your emotions; for organizations, avoid customer observations like the plague, particularly in offering design
7. Never Set Goals: for individuals, never set a direction for your life, let "life" happen; for organizations, avoid strategic objectives, especially if they involve understanding your customers
8. Focus on Outcomes: for individuals and organizations, make sure you are results-oriented instead of behavior-oriented. After all, staying busy is more important than focusing on

behaviors that are more likely to lead to success and winning is more important than how you play the game

9. Don't Give: for individuals and corporations, give as little as possible to help your family, friends, team, organization, community, or country become better
10. Don't be Fit: for individuals, be as unfit as possible so you can be as useless as possible to the greatest amount of people; for organizations, produce the lowest quality offerings the market will accept

How to Discover Purpose

Now that I've gotten the *via negativa* out of the way, here's what I know.

The first workplace intervention needed to lead engaged Millennials is to connect their purpose with your organization's purpose. And I don't mean the nonsense plastered on the lobby wall by the PR people—I mean the real reason you are in business. Since most people don't know why they exist, when they get together for a common end (be part of a company) they often do so for the lowest common reason: money. Whether wages or short-term profits, economic survival is often the real reason they all got together to begin with.

First, understand why your organization exists—who benefits from your activities, how do they benefit, and why they benefit. And focus on the linchpin—the one group without whom your organization ceases to exist. Most organizations exist to serve customers—even non-profit organizations—as the prime group, with employees in second place, and shareholders and stakeholders in third place.

The customer is whomever pays you for your offering (product or service). Shareholders and stakeholders are those who benefit from, but do not pay for, your offering. Employees are those whom you pay in order to produce and deliver the offering.

The customer is the sole reason your organization exists.

Without a customer, you will not need an organized group of individuals to work together to design, produce, and deliver your offering—and the shareholders and stakeholders really don't matter if there are no customers.

Second, make sure your real purpose is used to recruit people to join your organization and then reinforce the purpose connection between the organization's and employee's purpose. You may need to help them discover their purpose since most people live meaningless lives. But you can't help them until you've figured these things out for yourself and your organization first.

Your organization's purpose is rarely understood and often isn't real—at least the published purpose isn't. This causes an organizational, collective cognitive dissonance between what the organization says and what the organization does. For now, ignore the official purpose and get to the heart of why your organization really exists.

To discover what the true purpose of an organization is, there are four questions that need answers.

1. What is the organization best at, what are your core competencies?
2. Why was the organization created? (What problem do you solve, which need do you satisfy, what pain do you relieve, or gain do you create through your offering)
3. For whom do you create that difference (who is your customer)?
4. How does this organization's offering make a difference in the real world (why do your customers care and how much do they care)?

Once you've answered those questions honestly—and I mean with brutal honesty—you'll have an idea of the organization's true purpose. And a bottle of water doesn't inspire a moment of optimism and happiness unless you've first been driven insane by extreme dehydration.

Your organization likely has multiple offerings with different customers for each one—it is important to identify both the offering and the specific customer for the offering. Your customer may be a business (business-to-business or B2B) or a consumer (business-to-consumer or B2C). Businesses and consumers have different needs, different Jobs-To-Be-Done, and often different reasons for buying the identical offering.

Many organizations go about this all wrong—they develop an offering and then search for a market for it. These organizations are sales focused because they have to convince someone to part with something of value in exchange for the offering—selling.

Great organizations search for problems to solve, needs to satisfy, pains to relieve, and gains to create based on their core competencies. Once they've found such a thing (by the way, we are surrounded by them—they are called opportunities), they set out to deeply understand the context of the opportunity to see if a market exists for a solution—a solution that can be profitable for the organization to develop and produce.

To understand the opportunity, you must spend time observing the potential customers, interviewing them, and engaging them in testing your offering. They often don't know what they really need and have a terrible time expressing themselves—so what they do and why they do it is best observed than questioned. When you do question, make sure the question is open, not closed—never ask a question that can be answered with one word.

When you set out to discover the potential customer's why, you should discount the first reason they give and focus on the second or third reason. These are most often the real reason. I often discover that real reason by asking, "In addition to (fill in the blank), is there another reason you care about (fill in the blank)?"

How much they care about the opportunity gives you information about how much they value a solution—and lets you know whether this is an opportunity worth pursuing. We've developed an algorithm that allows us to capture and rank opportunities as well as describe the competitive landscape—all from the potential customer's perspective, which is the only perspective that matters.

After the true corporate purpose has been discovered, there are four more questions to be answered to bring clarity and usefulness to the purpose.
1. Is this purpose specific enough to defend?
2. What is set in stone and what is flexible as the environment changes around the organization?
3. What is the plan to defend this purpose against short-term perspectives and pressures?
4. Is the organization's purpose connected to your personal purpose?

Once you understand these questions and the insights generated into the minds of your customers (and potential customers), you will have a much better grasp on the real purpose of your organization. It also helps you capture your value proposition for each offering and customer.

How your customer benefits from your offering really provides insight into your organization's purpose. Now, you need to communicate that purpose up, down, and sideways throughout the organization.

As a leader, your job is to influence others to help you accomplish your purpose—this is a lot better if your purposes are similar, or even better, aligned. If your people don't know what their purpose is, it's in your best interest to help them discover it as quickly as possible. This way, you can figure out pretty soon whether there is a good fit between you or not.

If the fit isn't good, help them by letting them move on to another organization as soon as possible.

To discover personal purpose, these questions need answered.
1. What are you really good at?
2. What problems do you solve, pains you relieve, gains you create, needs do you satisfy in your operating space?
3. To whom do you matter?

4. How do you make a difference in their lives?
5. What makes you forget the world around you?
6. How can you get outside your comfort zone but stay in your strength zone?
7. How are you going to improve your operating space in this volatile, uncertain, chaotic, and ambiguous (VUCA) world?
8. What would you do with your time if you weren't allowed in your home between 8 am and 7 pm, weren't allowed to work and your children were taken care of?
9. What is your dream?
10. How can you make it happen?
11. As a child, what were your most memorable experiences?
12. Who is your role model and why do you admire them?
13. What are your core values and beliefs?
14. What causes are near and dear to your heart? How can you use your strengths to help?
15. What goals should you set for yourself?
16. What legacy do you want to leave?

If you really want to improve your life, take action and write your answers to these questions—and I mean all of them!

Start with YOUR answers to the corporate purpose questions. This will help you discover what YOU think the purpose is, not what the crazy people in the marketing department think it is. Don't just think about these answers—it is essential that you write them down.

After you've written your answers to those corporate purpose discovery questions, tackle the 16 personal purpose discovery questions. And please, for the love of all that is good and holy, write down your answers!

Writing (by hand, not typing on some digital device) creates a deeper connection between you and the content you just created. Since this content is about your life, framing what is important so you can focus on becoming the best version of you that your operating space needs, you should probably WRITE IT DOWN so you can be more deeply connected.

Or you can ignore me, do what 75% of readers do, live a passive life instead of take action, and spend the rest of your life wondering why it didn't get better.

How to Live a Life of Purpose

The first step to live a life of purpose is to become authentic. This demands intellectual honesty, emotional honesty, and self-acceptance. Remember, self-acceptance always trumps self-esteem. But in order to accept yourself, you need to know the true you—not your perception of yourself, but a true perspective. This, like life in general, is difficult.

We are biased and our self-assessments generally unreliable. A technique I use to mitigate my bias is to do a self-assessment, then have my staff do the same assessment on me. I average their scores, pay attention to the outliers, and discount my own scores. This gives me a more true perspective of who I am—and then I must accept it.

Self-acceptance, by the way, doesn't mean I must stay where I am if I don't like it. It means to accept where I am as a baseline for improvement. It's all about becoming better, not being better.

If you don't know where you really are, your destination doesn't matter; you'll never get there because you are plotting a course from a false starting point. This is one reason why many people never achieve the goals they set for themselves.

The second step to live a life of purpose is to become curious about yourself and your world—the space in which you dwell. Explore, not with the intent to exploit, but with the intent to understand. I like to discuss issues with people who disagree with me—not to shape them to my view, but to allow my view to be shaped and sharpened by seeing the world through a broader lens.

I like to put myself at the intersection of ideas and disciplines—as many as possible that are as different as possible—so I can learn as much as possible in the shortest time. While doing so, I try to avoid theorists and spend my time with practitioners with a record of expertise.

In my own areas of expertise, I learn as much as I can from people who are new to the domain. They see things with fresh eyes and ask questions the experts don't. This is key to avoid a practice built on assumptions held by experts.

The third step is to expand your potential by trying new things and practice, with deliberation, your strengths. You want to stay in your strength zone and out of your comfort zone. This exposes you to more opportunities to grow whilst maximizing the likelihood of success.

I like Earl Nightingale's definition of success: the progressive realization of a worthy ideal. This is best done by improving your strengths rather than your weaknesses. Step three builds on steps one and two—stay in your strength zone and out of your comfort zone.

The fourth step is to know your values and why you hold these values. I like what Dr. Russ Harris says: "Hold your values loosely, but pursue them vigorously!" Throughout your journey to a life of purpose, you will hold different values at different times. This is why you need to know what your values are and why you hold them at this time.

You get to choose your values. This is not the same as situational ethics, where your values depend and shift on the context of the situation. It is pre-determining your values and then living according to the values you have chosen. Your beliefs (values) precede your actions and your actions precede your emotions.

When your beliefs and actions don't line up, you will experience distress and have a choice to make to relieve the distress: change your actions to match your values, or change your values to match your actions. When your stated values don't line up with your actions, it is an indication that you aren't pursuing those values with vigor—your deeds speak volumes about what you actually value, so you have a self-perception that is self-deception.

Whichever choice you make, be intellectually honest with yourself—and live according to the values you have chosen. I recommend you check out the Values In Action website for an assessment that ranks your values in order of importance to you—and then have some other people who know you do the same assessment on you.

Your assessment is based on what you think—their assessments are based on what they see you do. This helps identify any areas of dissonance between what you think you believe and what your actions declare you to believe—your actions are a better indication of what you believe than what you say you believe. And change your actions to meet your values... it's a better option and more likely to succeed.

The fifth step to a life of purpose is to focus on the important. This is all about reducing, not expanding, the distractions in your life. Say, "No!" to the thousands of interesting things in order to say, "Yes!" to the few things that move the needle of your life in a positive direction. Your strengths and values will help you decide what is important—and what is not.

Simplify your life to the important and make sure you leave space in your life for reflection so you can make course corrections as needed—this is important.

The sixth step to a life of purpose is to be outward-focused and internally-aware. Mindfulness meditation is a way to be present in the moments we have with people, while we maintain an awareness of our beliefs, actions, and emotions. An outward-focus requires us to have an accurate assessment of what is happening in this moment—we need to understand the others around us before we respond, we need to be attuned to our environment, we need to be masterful observers of our surroundings and the people we spend our time with.

The seventh step to a life of purpose is to become ambitious. Ambition is a desire to achieve a specific goal—whether your ambition is creative (positive) or destructive (negative) depends on your goal. Goals are important because they help you maintain your focus on the important things in your life that will help you achieve your purpose in life. It starts with an honest, brutal evaluation of where you are now and where your life is headed—and then compare that with where you want to be.

Don't focus on outcomes as a benchmark for achieving your goals—focus on executing the behaviors that are likely to achieve the goals. Ask yourself what you would like to get out of your life, what you might get, and what might be attractive to get—and detail why.

Describe the behaviors you will need to engage in to reach your goals—what you are doing now isn't working. Otherwise, you'd already have the desired outcome or something similar—outcomes cannot be guaranteed because they rely on so many uncontrollable variables for success.

Determine what needs to happen in order to reach the goal—what do you need to change in yourself, what actions must you take—focus only on the things you control: your beliefs and values, your behaviors and actions, and your emotions and feelings. Work backwards from the desired end-state to your present-state, always asking, "In order for this to happen, what had to happen immediately prior to this?"

Focus on executing value-based behaviors, those values you determined in Step 4. Values will motivate you to persist in the face of setbacks, give you guidance in decision-making, and a sense of fulfillment as you progress through your purpose. Purpose is a journey, not a destination.

Be clear when you state the behaviors and actions you can do to optimize reaching your long-term goals. Your goals may progress from the functional through the emotional, through the life-changing, to the social impact you want to have. Specify these goals, not in terms of outcome, but in terms of behaviors and values you will perform. These must be measurable.

Some people like to use the acronym SMART—but I prefer SMARTER. These behavior and value-based goals must be Specific, Measurable, Achievable, Realistic, Time-bound, Evaluated, and Reviewed. You will have setbacks—nothing worth doing is easy—but you can minimize the frequency and size of the setbacks through short-term (weekly to 18 month) goal setting.

Don't limit your performance.

Life comes at you in waves so you will find yourself in periods of outstanding effort—take advantage of those opportunities! Hold yourself responsible; use an accountability partner or mentor to help you stay on track. Be self-disciplined: delay gratification, practice accepting responsibility, dedicate yourself to the discovery of truth, and balance yourself over the long-term.

The eighth step expands on the seventh: become behavior-oriented. Your life is full of choices, moment by moment. You can choose to react or respond, to feel or to act, to conform your beliefs or live the values you determine are important to you and your purpose.

At first, this will be difficult because you will separate yourself from your herd. You will experience the fear, even dread, of pulling away from your reference group and moving out of your comfort zone. But to live a life of purpose, you must do what the rest are unwilling to do: change. Practice behaviors and actions every day that reflect the values of the person you want to become—hold those values lightly, but pursue them with vigor.

Become relentless in your daily practices—choose each moment to respond by acting on your values.

The ninth step to a life of purpose is to give. Give to your family, your friends, your team, your colleagues, your community. Give, don't invest. Investors seek a return on that investment. Give your time, talent, and resources with zero expectations of getting anything back.

When you give and cannot get anything back in exchange for your gift, you change. You are becoming more than you are, expanding into your potential. You are transcending yourself.

Give to causes that cannot give you anything in return, and you will see a change in yourself over time.

The tenth step to a life of purpose is to become fit for your purpose. This means becoming physically fit (not Cross-fit), mentally fit, and spiritually fit to exceed the demands of your purpose. Warriors will have different needs than accountants or academics—so look at your purpose and determine the physical requirements needed to become fit in the areas of work, relationships, health, and recreation.

Beware of anyone pushing the latest fad (Cross-fit) or diet program…or if they claim to be a guru.

What are the mental requirements? Determine those and figure out where you are and where you need to be. Design and engage in the behaviors likely to get you there.

Spiritually fit isn't about religion. It is about the connection to things bigger than you. These are the activities that motivate you to become better, help you create your legacy, create a sense of community and belonging, provide hope, to realize your potential, and to help you expand into that potential.

Remember, it is about the behaviors and actions needed to get you where you need to be aligned with your purpose.

To recap, to live a life of purpose you need to:
1. Become authentic
2. Become curious
3. Expand into your potential
4. Know your values and why you hold them
5. Focus on the important
6. Become outward-focused and internally-aware
7. Become ambitious

8. Become behavior-oriented
9. Give time, talent, resources
10. Become fit for your purpose

Kenneth Frazier, CEO of Merck, said, "Leaders need to be purpose-driven, not personality-driven. If you don't believe in your company's intrinsic value or its contribution to society, if you're just focused on trying to make money, you're not going to be successful in the long run."

To become an effective leader of engaged Millennials, you will need to connect your organization's purpose to theirs—and you may need to help them discover theirs! And yours…

Get Good

Get Good

I'm pretty sure my dad never read Aristotle. My dad was from southern West Virginia, Logan County (Hatfield country), went into the Army, served in Korea, and settled in California where he met my mom. As far as I know, he only read Louis L'Amour books and the Bible.

He seemed to believe that child labor laws meant children were supposed to work, so when we were old enough to be useful, we went to work on his job sites. He was a third generation carpenter and homebuilder whose only marketing was word of mouth—which meant he had to be good, an expert. He focused on doing expert work and becoming better at it for a reason.

While my mom had the good Lord as her motivation (Do everything as unto the Lord), my dad had my mom. He worked with a craftsman's mindset, and insisted we did as well, because he wanted her to be proud of what he did and who he was.

Aristotle said, "Excellence is an art won by training and habituation. We do not act rightly because we have virtue or excellence, but we rather have those because we have acted rightly. We are what we repeatedly do. Excellence, then, is not an act but a habit."

While my dad never read Aristotle, he lived it.

He instilled in us the mindset of a craftsman. I have one brother who is a knife maker, another who is a cabinet maker.

I'm the odd duck out, not working with my hands anymore for a living—I work with people. And my marketing is word of mouth, like my brothers.

I applied the craftsman's mindset to everything I did, even when I fell into the Passion Trap (do what you love and the money will follow). It is, hands down, the best way to get good.

I collect mentors and coaches the way some people collect art. The difference is I don't sit around admiring my collection—I use them. Everything I've done, all the small (and large) career bets I've made, started with me learning the skills from the best I could find. Most of the places I've worked didn't have formal training programs—so I created my own informal program.

I sought out mentors and coaches who were best-in-class at what they did and studied them—how they thought about the work, and what they did.

I never shied away from the dirty work, the risky work. Thanks to Ben Rosson, I learned the best way to get through a minefield was to step in the footsteps of someone who has already made it across, but the best way to understand the minefield is to cross it first.

His point was that there are some things you only gain by doing and there will be times in your life when you're on point.

I've paid the price for doing work at the limits of my skills, outside my comfort zone. Sometimes that price is physical, sometimes mental, sometimes emotional.

I've wrestled guys who were way better than me—had my right shoulder completely separated and was knocked out with a German suplex in one bout—but I learned so much more when I was fighting for survival instead of beating guys who had no business calling themselves catch wrestlers.

When I have skin in the game, I become more aware of the situation, my thinking speeds up as I rely more on intuition, and I learn deeply—and I only have skin in the game when I take the risky option.

I improved my skills through deliberate practice and

performance—acquiring them through deliberate practice, mastering them through deliberate performance. At the time, I didn't know those terms existed—I knew this was the best way to learn and master new behaviors.

I had to teach myself how to identify a job, break it down into the component tasks, figure out what skills were needed to perform those tasks, and what I needed to know to help me understand the job better—and what I should do when things go pear-shaped. And they always go pear-shaped. I learned how to tell the difference between a theorist and a practitioner—and theorists may win arguments, but practitioners win.

I do first, then learn the theory underpinning what I did. Some people (like theorists) tell me I would learn more quickly if I learned the theory first—I've found I learn more deeply when I do what I do. One leads to shallow experiences, the other to deep expertise.

I had to get comfortable with being bored, but never boring. Becoming an expert at something is 98% pure boredom and 2% sheer terror.

One of the challenges we've seen in our education practice is the increase in teaching what is on the test. Another is the conflation of knowing about something with being able to do the thing. I don't like either of these concepts.

The people who only want to know the answers to test questions flounder when life changes the question—and life will always change the question. Instead of learning how to solve problems through reason, they memorized a response for a specific cue—and are now about as useful as Pavlov's dogs.

The conflation of knowing about something with the ability to do the thing is even more disturbing. It springs from the world of higher education, a world populated by theorists and researchers who teach from those very limited perspectives. Most courses should be taught by practitioners—but we are too busy doing instead of pondering what others should do, might do, or could do.

I've taught at a college before—as a practitioner in a very narrow field, I was the only person available in the region with the working knowledge and ability to teach. Most theorists don't know how to actually do the work, and so point to pieces of paper that attest to their slavery to the very world of academia that doesn't work. I've developed a heuristic around theorists: never learn from someone who has never made money doing the work in the private sector.

In the mode of *via negativa*, I will first discuss how to go about becoming mediocre, then switch to the mode of *via positiva* and reveal specific techniques I've used over the years to get good at what I do.

How to Become Mediocre

The first step to becoming mediocre is to know as little as possible. Make sure you only learn enough to earn enough which, if you followed my earlier advice, fits with Step Two of how to live a meaningless life. Mediocrity is ordinary and ordinary is meaningless—you are no better than the middle, the average.

Don't get me wrong—the world needs mediocre... somewhere, I'm sure. And the first step of the great leap to "meh" is to learn as little as possible.

The second step is to do as little as possible. Focus on living the passive life of observing, not doing.

I was on a camp-out with another family recently and saw a great illustration of this. The mother told one of her kids to sweep the floor of a pavilion. The kid stirred up quite a bit of dust. The mother then showed the kid how to sweep. The kid now pushed dirt in all directions. The mother then demonstrated how to sweep again, this time covering 75% of the pavilion floor. The whole time she swept, the kid watched. At the end of the ordeal, the mother had swept most of the floor while the child observed the mother do.

The child learned an important lesson: if you are mediocre, someone else will do the work while you watch them work. This cost of rework is huge to the company, but you shouldn't care—your goal is mediocrity, not operational excellence!

The third step to becoming mediocre is to tell everyone how much you learned in school, on the internet, or from books. After all, what you know and how well you can talk about what you know is more important than being able to do.

I've interviewed people for jobs and most of them seem fixated on their certificates attesting to what they know. When I put them up against the job they would do if hired, they fall down.

It turns out this is common.

I spoke with a manufacturer recently about their workforce challenges. They showed me two resumes from people they had recently interviewed for a welding position. Both individuals had a number of certificates that attested to their welding knowledge, certificates issued by a vocational school that had been paid thousands of dollars. These people could talk about welding—but when they were taken into the shop and asked to audition, they couldn't weld anything.

The good news for you—the labor market is in such dire straits (difficult position, not the band) that most employers don't ask you to audition before you get hired. And you can make a decent wage at mediocre (sometimes referred to as "C players"), especially if you can talk about how much you "know" instead of showing what you can do.

The fourth step to becoming mediocre is to learn from your peers. They don't know how to do the job with excellence, otherwise they wouldn't be your peer. So they are perfect people to learn from—because they can't do and can't teach how to do either.

Avoid people who have been doing the work for a long time, say about ten years.

You want to learn as little as possible from the new, the fresh, the people hip to the latest techno-babble, the ones fresh from the world of theories crafted by non-practitioners: your peers. This will also provide a unique experience; since they don't know any better (and you learned from them), they will tell you how good you are based on their own level of incompetence.

This will lead you to be incompetent, but thinking you are competent—and other incompetent people will reinforce that you are competent, when in fact you are not.

The fifth step to becoming mediocre is to only take easy assignments. Hard work, difficult work, is for suckers who don't know any better. After all, you didn't spend tens of thousands of dollars on a college education to work hard!

You are entitled to take it easy, and your place of employment needs to understand. You can shine, by the way, at doing easy work; a difficult assignment could make you fail—and everyone knows failure must be avoided at all costs.

Look around—who gets rewarded for failing, for making mistakes?

No one, that's who.

Make sure you don't risk failing—take easy assignments that are sure wins.

The sixth step to become mediocre is to focus on mindless, repetitive tasks—stick to what can be done with as little thought as possible. The predictable work is safe work, the routine work of everyday tasks are where the mediocre can excel at being ordinary.

In this modern age where most people worship the average, becoming good at these average, normal, table-stakes for employment tasks can earn recognition—or at least help you keep a job. Get good at the least important things and you can build a stellar career of mediocrity.

How to Get Good

Becoming excellent is simple, not easy. It requires effort, a willingness to risk failure, the desire to learn from practitioners who have gone before, and time. In this age of instant everything, many demand instant expertise and recognition for their unproven expertise (unproven outside the world of academia).

To become an expert takes time—you must make as many mistakes as possible in a very narrow field, according to physicist Niels Bohr. A true professional makes mistakes, recognizes them, and learns from them.

There are four specific ways to get good, and we must help Millennials get good at what they do if we are going to lead them—especially if we want them engaged with our organizations. These four ways to get good work together for optimal effect.

We need to provide them with a workplace mentor, or at least access to one. The mentor must be someone further along in their career, who knows the ropes, someone they can meet with on a regular, weekly basis and get advice from.

We need to teach them how to acquire new skills through deliberate practice. Deliberate practice is mindful practice that focuses on improvement in one element of the job and has a feedback loop built in, preferably with their workplace mentor.

We need to provide them with challenging work—at a

minimum, give them the opportunity to do challenging work. Challenging work will help them grow their skills.

We need to teach them how to master skills through deliberate performance. Deliberate performance is the mindful doing of the job with an eye to improve performance in the whole job, with the help of a coach.

Deliberate practice and performance are the main sources of expertise, and isn't the same as doing the work over and over again like a mindless drone.

Workplace Mentor

Mentors are not coaches—I've been, and continue to be, both. The essential distinction: mentors put learning into proteges, and coaches pull learning out of clients. As we've seen with work ethics, there is a clash between the "classical" and the "contemporary".

The classical definition of a mentor is someone with expertise who takes a personal interest in helping someone with less expertise become better in those areas of the mentor's expertise. This relationship is personal and exclusive, with the relationship deepening based on personal connections between the protege and the mentor; these connections are found through personality, profession, life-style, personal interests and hobbies, religion, and family background.

The contemporary definition of a mentor, the one preferred by Human Resource departments, is a leader who proactively develops their followers by helping them internalize their values, learn new skills, and master behaviors through the mentor's observation, assessment, coaching (ugh!), counsel, and evaluation of the protege. This relationship is formal, inclusive, and professional...and doesn't work.

Formal mentorship programs structured by HR fail to produce the long-lasting personal relationships needed for mentorship to succeed over time. A successful mentor-protege relationship is a rather unique blend of the personal and professional, blurring those boundaries and defying the rules set up by formal programs.

I've had the heads of HR departments tell me mentorship doesn't work—and they are sort of right. It doesn't work if it is set up by HR the way they do. They conflate and confuse good leadership behaviors or succession planning with mentorship, and then organize a program by targeting those who need it, defining mentor competencies, selecting mentors based on those competencies, matching mentors and proteges, developing mentoring guidelines, and training mentors in how to mentor their assigned proteges.

This has failed to produce positive results wherever it has been implemented—yet HR persists in this unproductive process because the alternative is outside their hide-bound control.

The mentor-protege relationship is one that can be initiated by either party, but it needs to be mutually agreed to. I had a client once that complained to me after I fired them that they had always considered me their mentor. I had no idea they considered me a mentor since we hadn't agreed to it and didn't do any of the things required for mentorship!

The job of HR is to ensure equal access to mentors, not play matchmaker, nor to ensure that all employees are treated equally by the mentors—ensure everyone has equal access to mentors. Or better yet, stay out of it and leave it to people who take the initiative to build this relationship. Proper mentoring is key to leadership development and should be encouraged and available, but never forced.

Mentors play at least ten different roles during the relationship with their protege. They will become tutor (in the Oxford style), guide, advisor, sponsor, role model, validator, counselor, motivator, protector, and the most important role—communicator. These roles enable mentors to develop leaders who can think and adapt to our volatile, uncertain, chaotic, ambiguous world, and empower proteges to become confident through behavior changes and performance improvement. These roles also allow mentors to shape corporate culture through the cultivation of corporate values in the protege.

When looking for a mentor, look for someone with about ten years more experience than you, that has expertise you want to have, and is about two levels up in the organization—don't restrict yourself to your direct line of command, but look for mentors across the organization in other lines of reporting or adjacent and related departments.

Mentors need to be competent, have a desire to help someone else, possess the ability to be non-judgmental, be a transparent communicator, an active listener, be trustworthy and respectful, have problem-solving skills, expertise in an area of interest to you (it's OK to have more than one mentor at a time), the ability to work on their own, and be organized and accountable. This list of required competencies rules out any notion of "peer mentoring", a concept that is completely useless. Mentors must be life-long learners.

When vetting a potential protege, they should be someone with a desire to become better, the ability to have open and non-judgmental conversations, an active listener, the ability to establish a relationship based on trust, the ability to work with autonomy under guidance, and must be responsible.

During this initiation phase, the prospective mentor and prospective protege must want to work together—the protege admires the mentor and the mentor believes the protege has potential and they would enjoy working with them.

During the cultivation phase, boundaries of the relationship are set. The protege must meet with the mentor on a regular basis (preferably weekly) and be transparent with their challenges and goals. The mentor helps the protege with those challenges and goals through guidance, feedback, and sharing the mentor's experiences, information, and access to their network with the protege. Access to the mentor's network isn't the same as patronage or nepotism. It is network accessibility, not promotion of the protege to the mentor's peers. The protege must be proactive and use the resources provided by the mentor's network.

Both mentors and proteges must keep aspects of their relationship confidential, except where required by law, organizational policies, and common sense.

The protege must be able to accept and act upon feedback provided by the mentor, and the mentor must be a positive role model for the protege. The protege should, with the mentor's help, identify and define professional and personal development goals. These SMARTER goals must be tracked and the protege held accountable for their actions toward their goals.

During this phase, the mentor must set high performance expectations. They need to offer challenging ideas to the protege, shift the context of the problem so the protege can see a positive outcome and identify worthy goals. The mentor must inspire the protege to move toward those goals and check their goal commitment level.

The mentor must listen empathetically, ask insightful questions, and not give advice unless asked. The mentor must encourage reflection and self-awareness, help the protege identify what motivates them and reinforce the protege's belief in their growth potential.

The mentor must confront negative attitudes and behaviors of the protege in a nonjudgmental way, without becoming destructive, and provide insight into unproductive strategies. The mentor must explain how the organization works, share useful information, provide guidance, present different perspectives to drive deeper analysis by the protege, and stimulate creative thinking.

The mentor should provide growth opportunities, encourage the protege to explore multiple options, and allow the protege to choose their own path and make it work.

Most of all, the mentor must become the protege's friend.

During the separation phase, the protege demonstrates

independence, autonomy, and maturity—it is time to find a new mentor. The current mentor has developed their protege as much as they can (for the most part). It is time to move on.

The mentor-protege relationship must be allowed to evolve.

The purpose must be revisited, feelings and concerns addressed, progress reviewed, experiences evaluated, and the nature of the relationship reflected upon. The mentor should help the protege find a new mentor, one who can help the protege develop further.

In the re-definition phase, the mentor and protege establish friendship as the basis of their relationship. They have built mutual trust so far, which makes it easier to treat each other as valued colleagues.

Mentoring is not a one and done, done and dusted deal. It is a virtuous upward cycle. The initial mentor hands the protege to a new mentor and the protege becomes a mentor.

Leadership is influence, nothing more and nothing less; the best way to influence someone is to add value to them.

I had a client tell me they were concerned about investing all this time, effort, and energy into developing their people; what if the organization does this massive investment, and the people become better and then leave for a competitor?

My response: what if you don't make the investment and they stay? Your workforce is your number one competitive advantage, your unique differentiator in the marketplace. Don't blow it with a myopic perspective!

Mentoring benefits the organization, no doubt about it—when it's executed properly with as little interference from HR as possible.

The accessibility of mentors makes it easier to recruit and onboard new talent. The new talent is acclimated to the work environment with ease, becomes more productive faster, and is less likely to leave because the organization has signaled a commitment to them. This reduces the cost of talent turnover.

The talent understands long-term plans more deeply, grasps

how their career can progress in the organization, has personalized development and improvement —all lead to higher positive engagement and discretionary effort. The organization gets the opportunity to identify and explore values gaps and manage corporate culture better.

Mentoring also helps the organization plan for succession. It is easier to identify training and development needs, get senior management a deeper understanding of the available talent pool, and provides the opportunity to recognize the aspirations and potential of the proteges.

The open channels of communication established through mentoring improves productivity as communication increases across teams and informally across organizational lines and boundaries.

Proteges benefit from mentoring because they have the opportunity (if they seize it) to link theory learned in school to practice—from a practitioner, not a theorist. They can discuss challenges with someone other than their manager, and gain access to a larger network from someone who believes in their potential.

They get help clarifying their goals, develop confidence, and learn how to deal with the structure of the organization. They learn tactics to help them become comfortable with a diverse range of people, and learn how to communicate with upper management.

They get to hear the voice of the organization's conscience as they learn to make decisions and take action based on the organization's values.

Mentors benefit through the experiential learning they undergo through the relationship. This gives them the opportunity to re-assess their thinking, broaden their perspectives through fresh eyes, and learn new ways to influence others not under their direct control.

This intellectual challenge sharpens their skills, and as a result —their reputation in the organization grows as they reinforce best practices and share their expertise.

There is an innate human satisfaction derived from helping someone who can't help you—the reflective space required for mentoring becomes a source of insight for the mentor.

Deliberate Practice

Deliberate practice is the second piece that leads you to become good at something. Deliberate practice helps you learn a new skill. The amount of time spent doing something (your years of experience) doesn't build expertise, the amount of deliberate effort expended over time does. That deliberate effort must be intentionally focused on improving your skills, whether the soft skills that are difficult to teach and learn, or the hard technical skills that are relatively easy to teach and learn.

Deliberate practice is required to learn new skills, challenging work is required to grow those skills, and deliberate performance is required to master them.

Deliberate practice activities are at the right level of difficulty for the protege. These activities must be challenging, and outside of their comfort zone. This requires the mentor to have a deep understanding of what the protege can already do—and can't do.

Identifying the skills gaps in the protege relative to their role is a crucial task—and not one that can be trusted through self-evaluation. Many people that have pieces of paper attesting they know things only know about them, not how to do them.

Your organization's competitive advantage lies in your people and their ability to execute your organization's core competencies in alignment with organizational purpose.

Deliberate practice activities must allow the protege to refine their skill through reflective repetition. The point is not to get the exercise over with so HR boxes can be checked off—the point is to have the protege perform the exercise with conscious monitoring and control. This is not designed to develop shallow, automatic responses.

This requires full concentration and effort.

Because this level of focus and effort taxes the mind and body, these exercises should be scheduled for the time of day the protege can deliver their best.

Deliberate practice activities give the protege room to make mistakes—and correct them. We learn through our mistakes and we do Millennials a great disservice if we set up rules that prevent them from making mistakes. Worse, we set them up to be crushed by reality when we tell them their substandard performance is good.

The modern culture has become obsessed with self-esteem—one of my sons told me once that my job as a father was to make him feel good about himself. I told him my job was to prepare him to have a difficult life—and the real world doesn't care about how you feel about yourself.

What matters most is self-acceptance.

Accept the truth of where you are, what you are currently capable of, figure out where you want to be, decide the values needed to get you there and act according to those values. You will make mistakes. Accept them, own them, learn the lessons, make the needed corrections, and go again.

Deliberate practice activities need a timely feedback loop built in, whether from an automated system or an observation from the mentor. The closer the feedback is to the time the mistake was made, the better the protege can synthesize the lessons to be learned and identify when they are about to make the same mistake.

Feedback isn't only about mistakes and opportunities to learn; when the protege does something well, the mentor needs to tell them in the same timely manner. Performance feedback, whether about things done well or lessons to be learned, is all about growth and that happens best when the action and feedback are close in timing.

Deliberate practice helps people become independent and better able to design their own deliberate performance activities to master the skills learned through deliberate practice.

Mentors need to design deliberate practice activities that are relevant to the protege's role in the organization. Since these are practice activities, not actual projects, the mentor needs to identify what is considered skilled performance on tasks that are part of the job.

The goal is to improve specific parts of the skill within the context of the entire skill.

For example, if solving problems is the skill the protege is learning, a case study relevant to their job could be used. The first step would be to define the problem (or problems) in a problem statement. The deliberate practice exercises would focus first on defining the problem, allowing the protege to gain skill in problem definition across multiple case studies before moving to the next task which is to write a clear and concise problem statement.

The mentors should also identify the performance criteria connected with the different levels of expertise in that role.

The level of focus and intentional effort during deliberate practice should preclude these activities from being scheduled for more than 2 hours at a time (preferably during the weekly mentor-protege meetings). If the protege isn't exerting that level of effort, the exercise isn't challenging enough.

Case studies and critical incident reports should be tiered so the protege can move up in level of difficulty to learn these required skills. This kind of organized knowledge is a lever for the organization to develop expertise in their people.

The key is to use case studies and critical incident reports that are relevant to the different roles of the proteges. This is an investment in your organization's competitive differentiation and your unique competitive advantage.

There are two techniques proteges can use to enhance deliberate practice.

The first is to orally explain what they are doing and why while performing physical tasks, and either orally or in writing after performing mental tasks. Self-explanation allows the protege to cement what they have learned by improving the neural paths associated with the tasks.

The second technique is for the protege to visualize task performance and the next steps. This will require a base understanding of how to do the task for optimal performance. Visualization has been the key for me to gain expertise across the many domains I've had in my career so far, and continues to be critical to my success in gaining new skills.

One colleague I've worked with for over a decade recently told me that my true expertise was in the acquisition of new skills. Visualization is my secret weapon.

We have to understand that experience alone does not provide expertise. Evaluated experience gained through deliberate practice and deliberate performance does. While experience does not guarantee expertise, expertise does require vast experience across a domain.

Another thing we must remember is that observation is not the same thing as doing. Watching a catch wrestling bout will not provide the same level of skills as getting in the ring does—and that holds true for every other profession I've worked in. Mindful practice and performance to improve makes all the difference.

Challenging Work

The third piece needed to get good is to provide them the opportunity to do challenging work. Don't assign the Millennial this work—encourage them to take these opportunities. This is a good way to see if they have the desire to improve. After all, no one becomes an expert by mastering the trivial and routine...or by reading three books on a subject.

Challenging work opportunities are at the boundaries of their comfort zones—and I mean on the other side of the boundary, not inside their safe space. The greatest growth always takes place outside our comfort zone—in order to find those boundaries, we need to know where they become afraid.

One of my mentors, Ross Bacon, hired me to lead one of his companies. About two hours into my first day, I felt overwhelmed and out of my depth. I felt the fear—I had never led a team that large before. I went into his office and told him "I don't think I can do this." I will never forget what he told me: "I hired you because I know you can do this. If you didn't feel like this, I wouldn't have hired you." He then went back to work—and so did I.

Ross knew something that William James had discovered over a century ago: "A new position of responsibility will usually show a man to be a far stronger creature than was supposed."

Challenging work is risky work. The opportunity will be loaded with risks: risk of reputation, job loss, financial ruin, failure, loss of physical and mental health, failure, loss of friends, loss of status, and did I mention failure?

If you don't have skin in the game, the game isn't worth playing.

Challenging work is so scary it will make you want to wear Depends to work.

Fear can be a healthy motivator to act or it can be a paralyzing force. People talk about the fight or flight response. It's actually the fight, flight, or freeze response.

The greatest risk is to freeze—to get caught in the paralysis of indecision. How you perceive failure makes the difference to how you respond to the risk of failure, and how you feel (excited or fearful). Remember, beliefs precede actions and actions precede emotions.

You will have to move outside your level (or even your area) of expertise to do challenging work. If it were able to be done with ease and expertise by you, it wouldn't be challenging work now, would it?

Stick to your strength zones, but extend yourself to the limits of your strength—to the space where you start to feel weak. Your skill sets may transfer across domain boundaries into areas you don't have expertise. These are the places that will cause you to grow.

One time I was asked to run a small boutique shop that sold art prints. I knew how to sell, I knew how to lead people, I knew how to manage a business—but I knew nothing about framing prints, cutting mats, and knew nothing about contemporary prints. I took the job and learned a lot. The skills I already had developed more, and I learned new skills.

Challenging work provides stimulating diversity to what you do. When you are in over your head, you find creative ways to get to the top or you drown. Life is too short to do boring work, and a great way to stay engaged is to work at jobs and opportunities that arouse your curiosity, inspire you to perform at or near your best, and make you feel alive.

Add value to Millennials by providing them with the opportunity to do challenging work.

Challenging work often involves working with other people. Honestly, that's where most of the challenge lies. Working with people across departments, roles, and functions will deepen your cultural understanding. It is, in this age, imperative that we preserve cultural differences through understanding that different is not the same as wrong. Promote cultural understanding—provide your Millennials the opportunity to work on challenging, cross-functional projects.

Challenging work will also provide greater visibility of the Millennials to senior management. Whether they win or lose isn't as important as they were seen by management as willing to risk failure. Good leadership recognizes that failure is key to learning and proves the worthiness to promote.

Show me a person who has never lost, and I'll see a timid soul who never learned. They may know about something, but they don't know it with intimacy. Good senior leadership will never consider failure a loss unless the wrong lesson is learned or no lesson was learned.

The only way to grow skills is to do challenging work. People who settle for the least never become the best. If all you do is the trivial, mundane, boring, routine work, your skills won't improve. You will get OK at doing work that can be automated by technology. In that case, robots can steal your job. But if you want to lead engaged Millennials, let them grow their skills when they volunteer to take on challenging work.

Deliberate Performance

The fourth piece to get good, deliberate performance, is similar to deliberate practice, but the focus is on mastering the entire skill, and sets of skills, required across the domain you work in. As you acquire your skills through deliberate practice, you master them through deliberate performance on real projects, not exercises. Deliberate performance requires the use of a coach, not a mentor; a coach who can pull learning out of the coaching client.

Deliberate performance can be used with skills that cross project boundaries (so the performance can be repeated across varied job contexts), needs timely feedback that doesn't require expert observation and judgment (your coach doesn't need to be an expert at doing the thing, but an expert at coaching), and must be applied to lots of different tasks that increase in the level of challenge.

A word or several about coaching: a coach doesn't have to be an expert at the stuff you do in order to be a great coach. They have to be a great coach. As Timothy Gallwey found back in the 1970's, coaching is all about drawing the client into their potential through good questions.

I've proven this concept: I once coached Mark Wuttke into juggling three balls, shower style, even though I can't juggle a damn thing. The expertise a coach needs is in coaching, not whatever it is that you do.

Our research has revealed global skills gaps in a number of industries—skills that are important to master if one is to live a difficult life well.

The top 5 skills business leaders tell me they wish their people were better at are leadership, critical thinking, problem-solving, emotional intelligence, and teamwork.

These are all areas that can see significant improvement through deliberate performance.

Deliberate performance is mindful performance of the skills needed to complete a project, with an intentional focus on improvement.

While deliberate practice requires reflection after the act, deliberate performance is reflection in action—to take the time to get a real feel for the nature of the skill needed, of the job at hand. It is action taken to see what happens, creation of hypotheses that compete—and the test of those ideas to see which is more appropriate, to refine the ideas and test them again.

This involves risk—but risks taken to improve your skills are worth taking.

Deliberate performance recycles past experiences with reflection on the results—a good coach enhances that reflection which helps you learn the lessons faster. Coaches also help clients with reflective sense-making, how the client communicates the explanation of actions taken and outcomes that occurred.

The coach should encourage the client to try new behaviors, see problems in different ways, seek out different types of feedback, to develop better self-understanding and situational awareness.

Get Good Wrap-up

The second workplace intervention needed to lead engaged Millennials is to help them get good at what they do. The four components to get good are mentorship, deliberate practice, provide challenging work, and deliberate performance.

These four elements work together as the employee goes through a structured on-boarding process to autonomous work, just as the first workplace intervention, alignment of purpose, takes them through recruitment and on-boarding.

Each intervention builds upon the previous one, expanding the Millennial's expertise and role, helping them grow into their potential, while helping your organization build the unique competitive advantage you have in the marketplace—your human capital.

Take Responsibility & Give Accountability

Take Responsibility & Give Accountability

I think it is important to have a guiding philosophy in life, a system of ethics to guide decisions and actions, and a general style of thought.

I've always admired the Greek classics: Aristotle's concept of eudaemonia, built on a framework of values that guide me—to live a virtuous life well.

I also know the power belief has in transforming my life—what I choose to believe determines my actions, and my actions determine my emotions. It hasn't always been so.

There have been periods of my life when I allowed my emotions to rule my life. I got caught up in domestic drama, corporate intrigue, political machinations, and just about everything else that can show up on an emotional roller coaster at the carnival of life. I made some bad decisions, did some terrible things (not illegal, just not what I should have), and learned some valuable lessons.

To regain control of my life, to live according to my values so I can fulfill my purpose, I had to do a hard reset.

I rediscovered the sayings of Epictetus, the idea of Aristotelian ethics, and the writings of William James. I reached back even further to the ancient wisdom of the Near East, and found a way to think about life that works. I had an attitude adjustment.

I took responsibility for my beliefs, my actions, and my feelings. No one can make me feel a certain way, a few people can influence my actions, and an even smaller number can influence my beliefs. But none of them can control me. I am a wolf among dogs.

My inner circle is tasked with giving me accountability for ownership of my beliefs, actions, and emotions. This gives me a 360 degree perspective on my life.

Epictetus said, "The other day I had an iron lamp placed beside my household gods. I heard a noise at the door and on hastening down found my lamp carried off. I reflected that the culprit was in no very strange case. 'Tomorrow, my friend,' I said, 'you will find an earthenware lamp; for a man can only lose what he has.' The reason I lost my lamp was that the thief was superior to me in vigilance. He paid however this price for the lamp, that in exchange for it he consented to become a thief: in exchange for it, to become faithless."

Epictetus took responsibility for the lamp being stolen and held the thief accountable for becoming a thief. Of the two, the thief paid the highest price for the lamp.

Since everything in my life is a consequence of what I believe, do, or feel, I am responsible for everything in my life. This is the hardest lesson to learn and the hardest lesson to teach.

It is one of the most difficult things I've ever done.

The third workplace intervention is like a coin: one side is responsibility, the internal act taken by a person, and the other side is accountability, the external act performed by another. You must own your beliefs, actions, and feelings and you need others to reinforce that ownership.

I do not understand the helicopter parents who rob their children of growth opportunities because they refuse to let their child be responsible for their own actions. When my oldest son, Donovan, was little, I would hold him up to the pantry shelf where the boxes of breakfast cereal sat. He picked the cereal he wanted to eat for breakfast, and if he decided he didn't like it—he still ate it because that was the consequence of his choice. That's how we trained our children.

So I do not understand parents who do not hold their child accountable for the child's beliefs, actions, and feelings—worse, when they interfere and rob their child of the growth they were destined for. This will only delay the lesson, a debt with compounding interest that the child will be ill-equipped to pay when it comes due. This is difficult to see in parents of young children, and painful to see parents of adults engage in this behavior.

One person I know has an adult child enrolled in one of the nation's military academies. For the past year, the cadet has experienced an illness, recently diagnosed as an autoimmune disorder that threatens their commission as an officer. The parent is engaged in a letter writing campaign on behalf of their child.

This robs the cadet of the opportunity to grow in the face of adversity—to learn how to thrive when life chucks a bucket of fecal matter on them, to become resilient because of the challenge. It is precisely the wrong thing to do.

This parental behavior is far too common, and is often seen as one of the hallmarks of the Millennial generation—the most protected, most medicated, and most entitled generation in history. Helicopter parents have always been with us, but never at the scale afforded by the affluence of modern life.

How to Avoid Responsibility & Accountability

The tactic of avoiding responsibility and accountability has been around for a long time.

Napoleon Hill wrote, "All your life you have been forming the habit of dodging the responsibility of making decisions, until you have come, now, to where it is well-nigh impossible to do so." He also wrote, "When things did not go to suit you, instead of accepting full responsibility for the cause, you have said, 'Oh, hang this job! I don't like the way "they" are treating me, so I'm going to quit!'" Carl Jung wrote, "You are what you do, not what you say you do."

In these three statements we find the keys to avoid responsibility and accountability: first, get as many people as possible to make as many decisions for you as possible; second, make as many external forces as possible responsible for your condition; third, convince people that it is your intent, not your actions, that matter.

The easiest way to get someone else to make decisions for you is to refuse to make any decisions. This obvious answer works because someone will generally step up and make a decision they consider to be in your best interest, or someone will make a decision for you in their own best interest. When they do this, they usually mutter under their breath, "If you want something done right, you'd better do it yourself!"

Either way, you win on two fronts: you didn't have to make

the decision and, if you don't like the consequences, you can complain…I mean hold them accountable for their behavior. This passive-aggressive behavior is so common it's hardly noticed by anyone other than the decision-maker and action-taker—and if you picked your pigeon well, you will have selected a neurotic who is very willing to take responsibility for your indecision decision.

Stay away from people with character disorders—they won't accept responsibility for anything!

The second tactic is also so common it is rare to be noticed anymore. For generations we've been training children that they aren't responsible for their condition—it's their parents fault. If we can't blame (or won't blame) the parents, we can always blame society.

I recently watched an episode of "Fallet" on Netflix—there was a scene where a Swedish police negotiator was trying to establish rapport with a criminal by holding society accountable for the criminal's actions. The criminal surprised everyone by taking responsibility for his actions, stating that people like him did what they did because they were assholes.

The reversal of the usual positions was funny, but highlighted how common this is: a British-Swedish crime series used it for comic relief! Because it is so common, you can do it and very few people will notice. And if someone does make a comment, label them as fascist, or some other kind of "-ist" to deflect attention away from you.

The third way is to convince everyone that it is your intent, not your actions, that matter. After all, the only person who knows your intent is you—and you can say whatever you wanted your intent to be after the fact without fear of challenge. Your defense if your intent is challenged: "What are you, some kind of mind reader?" This will put the challenger in their place.

After the fact, you can build a narrative that supports your good intentions, a narrative that explains your actions as unintended consequences of events over which you had no control and that in hindsight you can see how they could be misconstrued and at the time they seemed the right thing to do. A fine example of this is found in State of Alaska vs. Steve Baden, a state employee who misused government funds to create a non-profit he was later contracted (and even later hired) to manage.

The settlement states, "Mr. Baden maintains he did not intend to violate the Ethics Act with regard to the facts set out in paragraphs 1-39. Despite his belief that he did not intend to violate the Ethics Act, Mr. Baden acknowledges that his actions set out in paragraphs 1-39 resulted in violations of the Act." While he got caught, he only had to pay a $5,000 fine—and as long as you don't fiddle with company (or government) money, you probably won't get caught.

How to Take Responsibility & Give Accountability

In an organization, it is imperative that each person owns their actions taken to achieve the mission and for peers and leaders to hold them accountable for the same. Millennials need to understand that responsibility is painful because life is a series of difficult problems—and avoidance of the problem because it is painful is the surest way to some form of mental illness.

Carl Jung wrote, "Neurosis is the natural by-product of pain avoidance."

Become responsible for your beliefs, your actions, your feelings. When you give someone else that responsibility, you cede control of your life to that person—a pitiful form of self-induced slavery. If you want control of your life, to fulfill your purpose, you must take responsibility for those elements you have absolute control over: your beliefs, actions, and feelings.

As leaders of Millennials, this is likely the most difficult part of leadership. I know it is for me.

There is some confusion around accountability—some think it is micro-managing. I used to micro-manage, and insisted that everything be done exactly the way I would do it.

One of my mentors, Charles Ballard, suggested I would exhaust myself if I managed the minutia—he recommended that I set boundaries through systems and processes, but give the employees the freedom to deal with the procedures using their own best judgment. My role, he explained, was to hold them accountable for following the process. It was a tough transition for me, but a good one—our productivity increased. The lesson Charles (and Ross Bacon) taught me was the bottleneck is always at the top of the bottle.

To hold others accountable requires that you first give them clarity about what the desired end state is and why that end state is important, and who else is impacted by that end state and the work needed to get there.

Then give them the resources and authority needed to execute their role, along with the behaviors and values needed to guide those behaviors.

It is OK to be uncertain, but it is not OK to be unclear.

Make sure the Millennial has a clear vision of the expectations—and hold them accountable for making value-based decisions and taking action based on those decisions.

Do not hold them accountable for the outcomes—those are out of their control. If everyone does their part the desired outcome is more likely, but nothing in this life is guaranteed except death.

I like to have my team set their own deadline—I then hold them accountable for what they told me they would do. They have to make tough decisions based on priorities and they will learn that their expanded role deals with more intangibles which create more complex uncertainties.

Hold them accountable for their responsibility to act.

As their expertise grows, as they prove their performance, we must expand their boundaries and provide them a greater role with greater accountability. We must connect their performance (actions) to the expanded boundaries.

We also need to provide them with immediate recognition and feedback when they do something good…or not so good. Forget the feedback sandwich, by the way.

When you say something positive, then give some corrective feedback, then finish with something positive, it doesn't work. It makes the person who gave the feedback feel good about themselves, but the recipient discounts both the corrective feedback and the nice things you said.

Millennials need to learn to take responsibility and we need to hold them accountable. This is the essence of John Maxwell's Law of Empowerment.

The Law of Empowerment states "Only secure leaders give power to others." They must take responsibility for themselves, and we must hold them accountable for their beliefs, actions, and feelings.

When this happens, they gain control of their lives, across the domains of Work, Relationships, Health, and Recreation—and become more engaged with the purpose of the organization.

Conclusion

Conclusion

It seems that, since the dawn of time, each generation holds successive generations with a certain level of contempt. Social sciences are fraught with too many variables to make certain our conclusions and empirical evidence usually has too small a sample size to be relevant.

The Millennial generation has gotten a bad rap on two fronts: the idea that they lack a work ethic and they are lazy.

The first is not a generational issue, but a cultural one with the differences between affluence, personal development beyond economic necessity, and parental attitudes toward class distinctions that lead to the classical work ethic or the contemporary work ethic.

The second is how we view our identity in relationship to our work. Some of us create a culture of overwork that is unhealthy and view those who do not share our views as lazy or not dedicated enough. This is also not a generational issue, but a highly individual issue of self-acceptance and identity.

The solution to lead engaged Millennials is to connect their purpose with that of our organization, to help them get good at something rare and valuable, and teach them how to take responsibility for their beliefs, their actions, and feelings and hold them accountable for their behaviors.

This is more likely to produce an engaged employee who will improve the organization's unique competitive differentiation and only sustainable competitive advantage: your human capital.

It is often easier to get a concept by declaring what it is not rather than what it is. I have included tongue-in-cheek advice on how to do the opposite of what one should do—it is the reader's choice to determine your own path.

Since my first encounter with a Millennial in the workplace, I have spent over a decade studying them. The three workplace interventions that are table stakes for leading engaged Millennials works for all the generations in the workforce as well. And they are not new, either; these leadership principles can be traced back to the military.

Generations of leaders in this country were trained to be aligned in purpose, to get good, to take responsibility and hold people accountable for their behaviors through the military experience.

In the business world (and military), bad leaders lead from position or personality. Good leaders lead through influence gained by adding value to people who choose to follow you. I encourage you to put these workplace interventions into practice.

Don't be average.

Become better.

Add value to the Millennials who work with you by connecting your corporate purpose to their personal purpose, help them get good at what they do, teach them to take responsibility and hold them accountable for their actions. If you do these things, they will become your secret weapon to kick ass in your marketplace.

Suggested Reading

Suggested Reading

K. Anders Ericsson, Ralf Th. Krampe, and Clemens Tesch-Romer. "The Role of Deliberate Practice in the Acquisition of Expert Performance". *Psychological Review*, 1993, Vol. 100 No. 3, 363-406

Mark L. Ritter. "Senior Leader Mentoring: Its Role in Leader Development Doctrine." U.S. Army Command and General Staff College, June 1994

John C. Maxwell. *The 21 Irrefutable Laws of Leadership.* Published by Thomas Nelson, Inc. Copyright 1998 by Maxwell Motivation, Inc.

Gregg F. Martin, George E. Reed, Ruth B. Collins, and Cortez K. Dial. "The Road to Mentoring: Paved with Good Intentions", *Parameters Autumn 2002*, U.S. Army War College.

John C. Maxwell. *The 360° Leader*. Published by Thomas Nelson, Inc. Copyright 2005 by Maxwell Motivation and JAMAX Realty.

K. Anders Ericsson. "Chapter 38: The Influence of Experience and Deliberate Practice on the Development of Superior Expert Performance", *The Cambridge Handbook of Expertise and Expert Performance*, 2006.

Kevin S. Groves. "View from the Top: CEO Perspectives on Executive Development and Succession Planning Practices in Healthcare Organizations", *The Journal of Health Administration Education*, Winter 2006.

Thomas J. DeLong, John J. Gabarro, and Robert J. Lees. "Why Mentoring Matters in a Hypercompetitive World", Harvard Business Review, January 2008.

Thomas C. Reeves and Eunjung Oh. "Chapter 25: Generational Differences", *Handbook of research on educational communications and technology, 3rd edition*. Edited by J. Michael Spector, published by Lawrence Erlbaum Associates, 2008.

John C. Maxwell. *Leadership Gold*. Published by Thomas Nelson, Inc. Copyright 2008 by John C. Maxwell.

University of Wolverhampton. *A Managers' and Mentors Handbook on Mentoring*. 2009.

Pew Research Center. "Millennials: A Portrait of Generation Next", February 2010

J. M. Twenge. "A Review of the Empirical evidence on Generational Differences in Work Attitudes", *Journal of Business & Psychology*, 2010

Carol S. Dweck. "Even Geniuses Work Hard". *Educational Leadership*, Vol. 68, No. 1, September 2010.

Peter J. Fadde and Gary A. Klein. "Deliberate Performance: Accelerating Expertise in Natural Settings", *Performance Improvement*, Vol 49, No. 9, October 2010

John C. Maxwell. *The 5 Levels of Leadership*. Published by Hachette Book Group. Copyright 2011 by John C. Maxwell.

Sally Seppanen and Wendy Gualtieri. *The Millennial Generation Research Review*. Published by the US Chamber of Commerce. Copyright 2012 by the National Chamber Foundation.

Calling Brands. *Why Purpose is Everything to the Modern Workforce*. 2012

Gallup. "State of the American Workplace Report", 2013

Pew Research Center. "Millennials in Adulthood: Detached from Institutions, Networked with Friends", 2014

Harvard Business Review, "What Millennials Want from Work, Charted Across the World", 2015

Deloitte University Press. *Global Human Capital Trends 2015: Leading in the new world of work*. 2015

Carolyn Heller Baird. *Myths, exaggerations and uncomfortable truths: The real story behind Millennials in the workplace.* IBM Institute for Business Value, 2015

Deloitte. "Mind the gaps The 2015 Deloitte Millennial Survey"

J. T. O'Donnell. "3 Reasons Millennials Are Getting Fired", inc.com, August 4, 2015.

Deloitte University Press. *Global Human Capital Trends 2016, The new organization: Different by design.* 2016

Victoria Hoffman. "Millennials in the Workplace". Docebo, 2017.

Self-Publishing School

NOW IT'S YOUR TURN

Discover the EXACT 3-step blueprint you need to become a bestselling author in 3 months.

Self-Publishing School helped me, and now I want them to help you with this FREE WEBINAR!

Even if you're busy, bad at writing, or don't know where to start, you CAN write a bestseller and build your best life.

With tools and experience across a variety niches and professions,
Self-Publishing School is the <u>only</u> resource you need to take your book to the finish line!

DON'T WAIT

Watch this FREE WEBINAR now, and
Say "YES" to becoming a bestseller:

xe172.isrefer.com/go/sps4fta-vts/bookbrosinc651

About the Author

About the Author

Since an inspiring Aha! moment as a child involving a sled, a snowy slope, and a bucket of human waste, Brett has been intensely curious about how the world really works—not from theory, but grounded in practice.

From his childhood on a primitive farm in the Canadian wilderness, where his family read <u>Little House on the Prairie</u> for survival tips, to his 7-year "overnight success" journey to the top of a niche industry, Brett leads through influence. He is considered by his peers to be one of the nation's top experts in sustainable residential construction and development.

A former surveillance operative, bodyguard, youth pastor, professional catch wrestler, and home builder, Brett is a polymath who leads a diverse team at The Dillon Group, Inc., an organizational development firm specializing in leadership development, competitive insights, quality management, and workforce development.

Brett and his wife have raised four sons and live in South Central Texas.

Brett is available for speaking and teaching engagements. Please visit our website, www.thedillongroupinc.com, for more information or email us at info@thedillongroupinc.com.

www.ingramcontent.com/pod-product-compliance
Lightning Source LLC
Chambersburg PA
CBHW020440220526
45464CB00002B/784